**DATE DUE
REMINDER**

Please do not remove
this date due slip.

Understanding the Elements of the Periodic Table™

BORON

Rick Adair

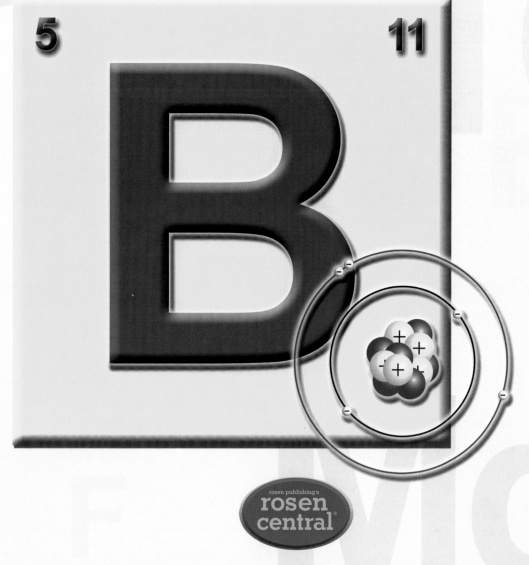

5

11

B

rosen publishing's
rosen
central®

New York

For Susan, Zach, and Devin

Published in 2007 by The Rosen Publishing Group, Inc.
29 East 21st Street, New York, NY 10010

Library of Congress Cataloging-in-Publication Data

Adair, Rick.
Boron / Rick Adair.—1st ed.
p. cm.—(Understanding the elements of the periodic table)
Includes bibliographical references and index.
ISBN-13: 978-1-4042-1004-2
ISBN-10: 1-4042-1004-0 (library binding)
1. Boron. 2. Chemical elements. 3. Periodic law—Tables. I. Title.
QD181.B1A285 2007
546'.671—dc22

                                                                2006023823

Manufactured in the United States of America

On the cover: Boron's square on the periodic table of elements. Inset: The atomic structure of boron.

Contents

Introduction

Francis Marion Smith, dubbed "Borax" Smith and the "Borax King," was a Wisconsin farm boy who went west in 1867. He had just turned twenty-one and wanted to make a fortune in gold or silver. He made it instead with borax, a boron compound. His wealth did not happen overnight, however. He wandered for five years across the territories west of the Rocky Mountains, prospecting when he could and working odd jobs when he had to.

Smith's big break came in 1872. He was cutting wood at Columbus Marsh, Nevada, for a San Francisco–based borax company. The marsh was in the middle of nowhere, about halfway between Las Vegas and Reno. His job was to fuel the boilers for the vats that refined ulexite ore, a source of boron and oxygen compounds called borates. The ore, called "cottonball" for its fluffy white appearance, was collected from the surface using rakes and brought to the vats.;

Curious about the bright whiteness of Teel's Marsh fifteen miles (twenty-four kilometers) to the northwest, Smith found a much richer cottonball field. Until then, the marsh had served as a source of sodium chloride (NaCl), or common table salt, used mostly for refining gold (Au) and silver (Ag) from Nevada mines. Smith staked a claim and set up a borax refinery at the edge of the marsh with his brother. Their find was so prolific and high-grade that in their first year of operation, they doubled the

Boron is a soft nonmetallic element that has both crystalline and amorphous (uncrystallized) forms. The black brittle solid shown here is boron's most common crystalline form.

country's output of refined borax. Within five years, his company was using mule teams to haul thirty-ton (twenty-seven metric ton) loads of refined borax 160 miles (258 km) north to Wadsworth, Nevada. There, the borax was loaded onto the recently completed transcontinental railroad for distribution in San Francisco, California. Until Smith's find, borax had been costly and used as a ceramic glaze or a flux (a substance used to help metals or minerals fuse together) for working precious metals. Teel's Marsh made borax a common household product.

Smith then set out to expand his holdings. He bought out his brother in 1884 and then gained control of all major borax production in western Nevada. Six years later, in 1890, he acquired borax operations in Death Valley, California, from William Tell Coleman and combined them with his own to form the Pacific Coast Borax Company. The company established its familiar 20 Mule Team trademark in 1891, inspired by the mule teams Coleman's company used to transport borax out of Death Valley.

After huge deposits of boron compounds were discovered in Nevada and California in the late nineteenth century, the once-rare substances became common enough to be used as laundry and cleaning products.

By 1900, Smith was very wealthy. In the turbulent economic years that followed, he lost his fortune, made another, and lost that as well. But the company this farm boy launched in the Nevada desert rose to become an economic powerhouse that today continues to mine borax and produce boron compounds as a subsidiary of the British mining conglomerate Rio Tinto.

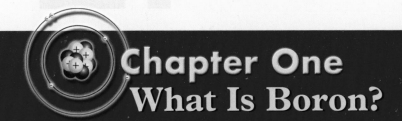
Elemental boron (B) is a light element with several forms that differ in the way the atoms are packed, none occurring in nature. The element is most familiar in compounds used to make fiberglass, heat-resistant borosilicate glass, and cleaning products. However, its most important role on Earth is as an essential micronutrient for plants.

The element is a rare portion of Earth's crust, representing only about seventeen atoms out of every million, although it is about 57,000 times more common in rocks than gold. Boron is found in more than 200 minerals, but only twelve are commercially significant, and only four satisfy nearly 90 percent of the boron demand.

Besides glassware and cleaning products, boron and its compounds have been used in semiconductors, fire retardants, cancer treatment, high-energy fuel, cosmetics, adhesives, pesticides, wood preservatives, and the leather tanning industry. Boron is also an essential part of Silly Putty. Other boron compounds are used as abrasives, in pyrotechnic flares, fiber optics, and advanced aerospace structures.

The Discovery of Boron

Elemental boron was isolated in an impure form in 1808 by French chemists Joseph-Louis Gay-Lussac and Louis-Jacques Thénard, and independently

Elemental boron was first isolated in 1808 by French chemists Joseph-Louis Gay-Lussac *(left)* and Louis-Jacques Thénard, and independently by English chemist Humphry Davy *(right)*.

by English chemist Humphry Davy. They all isolated boron by combining boric acid (H_3BO_3) with potassium (K). Gay-Lussac and Thénard called it *bore*, which is still its name in the French language.

Davy, thinking the new substance had metallic properties, proposed the name boracium, which combined "boracic" (the older form of "boric") with the Latin "ium" ending that indicates a metallic substance. However, after chemists determined it was not a metal, the new element was called boron in 1812. The name partly combines "borax" and "carbon" (C), element 6 in the periodic table.

Although boron is a relatively recent discovery, boron compounds have likely been known for a few thousand years, probably first through the compound borax, which can today be bought in many grocery stores for a relatively small price. But until 1865, when vast deposits in Turkey and California were discovered, borax was costly and hard to find.

Early borax deposits were found in dry lakebeds in Tibet, where it was known as tincal, from its Sanskrit name. It was transported in bags tied to sheep that were driven over the Himalayas into India. Many civilizations have an old term for borax—*nitron baurak* in Greek, *borith* in Hebrew, *baurack* in Arabic, *boreck* in Persian, and *burack* in Turkish. However, all seem to be transliterations of the Arabic word meaning "to glitter or shine," and there is no way to verify if they all referred to the same substance.

Wagons like the one shown here were hitched to mule teams and used to haul refined borax from Death Valley, California, to rail stations. The rear wagon carried a water tank.

In early Egypt, the mummification process—used by commoners and kings alike—included a soaking in the sodium (Na) ore natron ($Na_2CO_3 \cdot 10H_2O$). The ore often includes traces of boron compounds that would have been useful as a disinfectant and insecticide. Other boron compounds are thought to have been used in glassmaking in ancient Rome and in glazes in China from AD 300.

The first verifiable use of boron compounds was around 1,200 years ago, in Islamic countries. Some 200 years later, boron-bearing glazes were being used on ceramics made in China. Marco Polo brought borax back to Italy from the Far East in the thirteenth century, and borax was soon being imported into Europe from Tibet in small and expensive quantities. In Europe at the time, borax was mainly used in the precious metal trade as a soldering agent and for metal refinement.

The earliest reference to glass made with borax comes from China, in written descriptions of glassmaking by Arabs and others in 1225. The earliest European mention of borax in glass occurs in a German work in 1679 on recipes for artificial gems.

In 1777, boric acid, used today as a disinfectant and eyewash, was recognized in the hot springs near Florence, Italy. A rare mineral from the area, sassolite (H_2BO_3), was the main source of European borax from 1827 until 1872, when U.S. sources replaced it. Over the next eighty years, increasingly productive and vast borax sources were found in Nevada and California, most recently in the Mojave Desert. However, Turkish sources have grown since 1865 to surpass U.S. sources of boron compounds.

Boron and the Periodic Table

All ordinary matter in the universe is made of elements and combinations of elements. There are 111 elements confirmed and officially named today, and a few more awaiting verification or naming. Of the 111, 92 are found on Earth, 3 are found only in stars, and 16 are artificial.

Although each element is unique, chemists over the ages have noticed that some behave like others, especially in the way they combine with other elements.

There have been many attempts to organize the elements according to these chemical similarities. This is done today using a chart called the periodic table of elements, which is based on the work of Russian chemist Dmitry Mendeleyev and others. Mendeleyev introduced his first periodic table in 1869, which listed the sixty-three elements known at that time in order of increasing weight. He broke the element list into several clusters and displayed them so that chemically similar elements lined up. This arrangement was "periodic" because it highlighted chemical behaviors that repeated periodically. Although his original version arranged the elements in columns, with the lightest ones at the top and heaviest ones at the bottom, he eventually settled on a design that used rows, with element weights increasing from left to right.

Although the periodic table provides us with a useful summary of element properties, it was also once a powerful tool for predicting the existence of

Atomic Weights

Dmitry Mendeleyev's periodic table was especially successful because he had accurate atomic weights. He owed this to Italian chemist Stanislao Cannizzaro. In 1860, Cannizzaro cleared up the decades-long confusion about atoms and molecules by realizing that molecules can contain more than one atom. Confusing atoms and molecules can lead to overestimates of atomic weights. It would be like weighing a carton containing a dozen eggs, but thinking it contained only one egg. Cannizzaro relied on the work of fellow citizen Amedeo Avogadro from fifty years earlier that had been poorly understood at the time and, consequently, ignored.

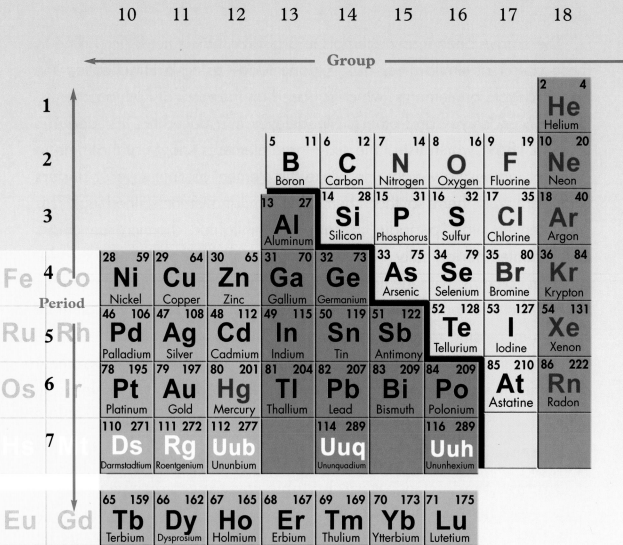

	VIIIB	IB	IIB	IIIA	IVA	VA	VIA	VIIA	O
	10	11	12	13	14	15	16	17	18

Group

Period

2	4
He	
Helium	

5 11	6 12	7 14	8 16	9 19	10 20
B Boron	**C** Carbon	**N** Nitrogen	**O** Oxygen	**F** Fluorine	**Ne** Neon

13 27	14 28	15 31	16 32	17 35	18 40
Al Aluminum	**Si** Silicon	**P** Phosphorus	**S** Sulfur	**Cl** Chlorine	**Ar** Argon

28 59	29 64	30 65	31 70	32 73	33 75	34 79	35 80	36 84
Ni Nickel	**Cu** Copper	**Zn** Zinc	**Ga** Gallium	**Ge** Germanium	**As** Arsenic	**Se** Selenium	**Br** Bromine	**Kr** Krypton

46 106	47 108	48 112	49 115	50 119	51 122	52 128	53 127	54 131
Pd Palladium	**Ag** Silver	**Cd** Cadmium	**In** Indium	**Sn** Tin	**Sb** Antimony	**Te** Tellurium	**I** Iodine	**Xe** Xenon

78 195	79 197	80 201	81 204	82 207	83 209	84 209	85 210	86 222
Pt Platinum	**Au** Gold	**Hg** Mercury	**Tl** Thallium	**Pb** Lead	**Bi** Bismuth	**Po** Polonium	**At** Astatine	**Rn** Radon

110 271	111 272	112 277		114 289		116 289
Ds Darmstadtium	**Rg** Roentgenium	**Uub** Ununbium		**Uuq** Ununquadium		**Uuh** Ununhexium

65 159	66 162	67 165	68 167	69 169	70 173	71 175
Tb Terbium	**Dy** Dysprosium	**Ho** Holmium	**Er** Erbium	**Tm** Thulium	**Yb** Ytterbium	**Lu** Lutetium

97 247	98 251	99 252	100 257	101 258	102 259	103 262
Bk Berkelium	**Cf** Californium	**Es** Einsteinium	**Fm** Fermium	**Md** Mendelevium	**No** Nobelium	**Lr** Lawrencium

The periodic table organizes elements in a powerful way. Each column (group) includes elements that combine in similar ways, while atomic number and proton count increase along a row (period).

elements. Most famously, in 1871, Mendeleyev predicted the existence of three elements and their basic properties. Within fifteen years, elements were discovered (gallium [Ga], scandium [Sc], and germanium [Ge]) that closely matched his predictions.

Today, the periodic table arranges the elements in a grid of rows and columns according to, first, the number of protons in their nucleus (the atomic number) and then the valence electron configurations. Together, these determine an element's properties. Each column, called a group, contains elements with similar chemical behaviors because they have similar outer valence electron configurations. The rows, called periods, list elements according to the atomic number and the filling of particular electron shells and sub-shells.

Each entry on the periodic table gives an element's name and chemical symbol, as well as the atomic number and atomic weight. The atomic weight is the average mass of the element's isotopes, as they occur naturally on Earth, reflecting the abundance of each isotope. The isotopes of an element all have the same number of protons but differ in the number of neutrons. The atomic weight is given in terms of atomic mass units, also called daltons. An atomic mass unit (amu) is defined to be one-twelfth the mass of a carbon-12 atom and is very close to the mass of a proton or one atom of hydrogen.

Boron's atomic number is 5, and it heads group IIIA (also called group 13). Its chemical symbol is B. Also in this group are aluminum (Al), gallium, indium (In), and thallium (Tl), which are all more metallic than boron.

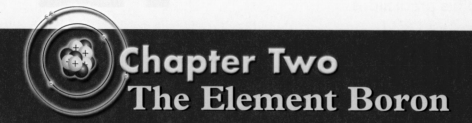

Chapter Two
The Element Boron

An element is made up of only one kind of atom and can't be broken down any further without losing what makes it unique. Inside the atom are smaller pieces called subatomic particles.

Subatomic Details

Boron atoms are so small that about 150 million of them laid side by side would span only an inch (2.54 centimeters). The pieces of an atom are even smaller. Although many subatomic particles are known, only three of them—protons, neutrons, and electrons—are important for understanding the basics of chemistry.

At the heart of the atom is a nucleus packed with protons and neutrons. Protons have a positive electric charge and are slightly lighter than neutrons, which carry no charge.

Electrons are more than 1,800 times lighter than a proton but carry a negative charge that is as strong as the proton's positive charge. In a neutral atom—one that has no net charge—there are as many electrons as protons. The electrons are found far from the nucleus, moving in complex ways. They can only move in "shells" that correspond to a set of specific energies. The number of electrons allowed in a shell is limited. When a shell fills up, electrons move to the next one. The first shell is nearest to the

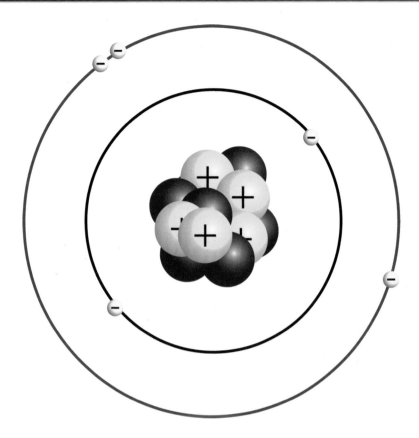

Boron atoms have five protons (yellow spheres) in the nucleus and five smaller electrons orbiting the nucleus. About eight of every ten boron atoms have six neutrons (dark spheres) in the nucleus, and the rest have five.

nucleus and can hold two electrons, while the next shell can hold eight electrons distributed among two sub-shells, one that holds two electrons, and the other that holds six.

Elements and Atomic Structure

The property of an element that makes it different from any other element is the number of protons in its nucleus. This controls the typical number of electrons and neutrons the element has. The arrangement of the electrons, in turn, affects how elements combine with one another.

15

Boron $^{5}_{11}$ B Snapshot

Chemical Symbol:	B
Classification:	Metalloid
Properties:	Very hard in crystalline form, brittle
Discovered By:	Independently in 1808 by Joseph-Louis Gay-Lussac and Louis-Jacques Thénard in France, and Humphry Davy in England
Atomic Number:	5
Atomic Weight:	10.811 atomic mass units (amu)
Protons:	5
Electrons:	5
Neutrons:	5 (B-10), 6 (B-11)
Density At 68°F (20°C):	2.34 grams per cubic centimeter (g/cm³)
Melting Point:	3,769°F; 2,076°C
Boiling Point:	7,101°F; 3,927°C
Commonly Found:	Boron isn't in nature in elemental form. It occurs combined as borax, boric acid, kernite, ulexite, colemanite, and tourmaline, and in borates. Large deposits of borax are in the Mojave Desert in Southern California. Boric acid is in volcanic springs and fresh and ocean water.

An element's properties categorize it as a metal, metalloid, or nonmetal. There are reflected in its proton count and electron configurations. The difference of a few protons can lead to dramatically different properties. Metals tend to lose some of their electrons, while nonmetals tend to pick some electrons up or share electrons with other elements. All metals (except mercury [Hg]) are solid at room temperature, good conductors of heat and electricity, and are generally easy to hammer into shapes (malleable) or draw out into wires (ductile). Nonmetals have properties that are very different from those of metals. They can be found as gases, solids, or liquids; are poor conductors of electricity and heat; and are brittle and not easily worked into shapes or wires. Metalloids have combinations of metallic and nonmetallic properties.

Boron, a metalloid, has five protons. The element with six protons is carbon, a nonmetal that is the basis of all life as we know it, while the element with four protons is beryllium (Be), a metal.

Another Visit with the Periodic Table

Mendeleyev's periodic table listed elements in order of atomic weight. Although this arrangement allowed him to find patterns of chemical similarity, it failed in a few cases. For

English physicist Henry Gwyn Jeffreys Moseley used his X-ray studies of atomic structure to more accurately place the elements in the periodic table by using the positive charge of the nucleus.

example, when the gas argon (Ar) was discovered in 1894, its atomic weight of 39.95 placed it after potassium, with an atomic weight of 39.10, and broke the pattern that grouped potassium with sodium and lithium (Li). But the pattern was restored twenty years later when Henry Moseley showed that the atomic number gives the positive charge of the nucleus and that listing elements in order of atomic number instead of atomic weight keeps the periodic table in complete agreement with chemical properties.

Like Mendeleyev before him, Moseley successfully predicted three elements using the periodic table, but based on atomic number, not atomic weight. These had atomic numbers 43 (technetium [Tc], discovered in 1937), 61 (promethium [Pm], discovered in 1945), and 75 (rhenium [Re], discovered in 1925).

The reason Mendeleyev's grouping by atomic weight worked fairly well is because a nucleus generally has at least as many neutrons as it has protons. Since protons and neutrons weigh about the same, ranking elements in order of atomic number (proton count) gives the same result as ranking

Atomic Number

Before 1913, nobody was sure what the atomic number meant. At the time, it was only an element's rank when ordered by atomic weight. In 1913, English physicist Henry G. J. Moseley showed that the atomic number gave the positive charge of the nucleus. Showing that this is the proton count had to wait until the 1932 discovery of neutrons in the nucleus. Until then, many scientists thought an element's atomic weight was due to protons and electrons in the nucleus. In this view, the protons provided most of the mass, and the electrons neutralized enough protons to provide the overall positive charge.

in order of atomic weight (essentially the total mass of the nucleus) in most cases. In a very few cases, weight-ranking reverses the ordering, as it does for argon, with eighteen protons and twenty-two neutrons, and potassium, with nineteen protons and twenty neutrons.

Columns and Valence, Periods, and Shells

The periodic table's groups, or columns, contain elements that combine in similar ways with other elements. For example, one atom of any alkaline earth element, including beryllium, combines with one atom of oxygen (O), whereas two atoms of alkali metals combine with one atom of oxygen. Some elements such as the alkali and alkaline earth metals always combine with another element in the exact same ratio. Others can form more than one compound with another element. These compounds have different ratios of the two elements and have different structures, as well as physical and chemical properties.

These chemical properties depend on the valence electrons, which are the electrons in the outermost energy level of an atom. Valence electrons can be lost, gained, or shared, depending on the nature of the element. The alkaline earth metals have two valence electrons. Elements that follow this sort of simple pattern are labeled with the valence in Roman numerals and an "A." These are called main group elements. Boron's group is IIIA, and all the elements in this group have three valence electrons.

Mendeleyev knew about valence, or the tendency of elements to combine in specific ratios, and this was how he grouped the elements. However, he didn't know that electrons were responsible for valence. In fact, he didn't know about electrons at all—they were discovered thirty years after he published his first table.

Mendeleyev's periods—the rows of the table—correspond to different shells. Boron is in period 2, so it has two electron shells. Because it is in group IIIA, we know there are three valence electrons in the outermost

Group Number

As more was learned about the behavior of electrons in atoms, the correspondence between periodic properties and valence electrons became clearer. It also became more complicated because of additional kinds of sub-shells that begin to fill up in elements belonging to period 4 of the table, starting with scandium. The International Union of Pure and Applied Chemistry decided to label the columns to bring the periodic table into accord with the modern understanding of electron structure in atoms. Rather than having "A" and "B" columns with Roman numerals, the column labels increase from Arabic numerals 1 through 18, specifying the total number of electrons added since the last noble gas element.

shell. Within each period on the table, the number of electrons in the shells increases from left to right across the row.

The heavier elements progressively fill other kinds of electron sub-shells that allow them to combine in more than one way with oxygen and other nonmetals. Elements with electrons in one or more of these other sub-shells are transition metals (in group columns labeled with "B"), and the lanthanide (La) and actinide (Ac) series (in the bottommost rows).

A Closer Look at Groups

Boron sits at the top of a stair-stepping band that ends at element 85, astatine (At). This band contains all of the elements diagonally down from B to At, as well as the elements germanium, polonium (Po), and antimony (Sb). The elements within this band are metalloids. Those to the left of this band on the periodic table are metals. All the metals are solid at normal

								He
				5 11 **B** Boron	C	N	O	F	Ne
				Al	14 28 **Si** Silicon	P	S	Cl	Ar
Co	Ni	Cu	Zn	Ga	32 73 **Ge** Germanium	33 75 **As** Arsenic	Se	Br	Kr
Rh	Pd	Ag	Cd	In	Sn	51 122 **Sb** Antimony	52 128 **Te** Tellurium	I	Xe
Ir	Pt	Au	Hg	Tl	Pb	Bi	84 209 **Po** Polonium	85 210 **At** Astatine	Rn
Mt	Ds	Rg	Uub		Uuq		Uuh		

Gd	Tb	Dy	Ho	Er	Tm	Yb	Lu
Cm	Bk	Cf	Es	Fm	Md	No	Lr

Elements in the highlighted diagonal band are metalloids, meaning they have both metallic and nonmetallic properties. Elements left of the band are metals, while those to the right are nonmetals.

conditions (except for mercury), shiny in appearance, good conductors of heat and electricity, and generally ductile and malleable.

Elements to the right of the metalloid band are nonmetals. The solid nonmetals are brittle, poor conductors of heat and electricity, not malleable or ductile, and tend to gain electrons in chemical reactions.

Chapter Three
Boron's Properties

All matter has characteristic properties that help identify it. Physical properties can be detected without transforming one substance into another. For example, melting a piece of boron changes it from a solid to a liquid, but it is still boron, so the melting temperature is a physical property. Other properties may be chemical. Chemical properties involve the way a substance changes (or doesn't change) in reaction to other substances. The way an element combines with other elements is controlled by the valence electrons; this is a chemical property. Finally, boron has nuclear properties—features of its nucleus—that set it apart from other elements.

Physical Properties

Pure, elemental boron, which is never found in nature, has several forms. Amorphous (uncrystallized) boron is a dark brown powder, while crystalline boron, a brittle solid, comes in many different crystal structures, including black, red, and yellow. The properties cited in this section refer to the element's most stable form, the black crystalline structure called beta-boron.

As a metalloid, boron does not conduct electricity or heat as well as a metal like copper (Cu), but boron conducts better than a nonmetal such as sulfur (S). If you were to hold a lump of the crystalline form of boron in your hand, it would feel a bit lighter than a typical rock of the same size. This measurable property of a substance is called density, which tells us how much mass we can fit into a standard volume. In chemistry, density is given in grams per cubic centimeter. Boron's density at room temperature is 2.34 g/cm^3. In comparison, the density of pure water is 1 g/cm^3.

The melting point of boron is 3,769°F (2,076°C), and its boiling point—the point at which liquid boron turns into a vapor—is 7,101°F (3,927°C).

Crystalline boron has exceptional hardness, ranking 9.3 on the Mohs' 10-point hardness scale. The Mohs' scale was invented to rate mineral hardness, and ranges from 1 for talc to 10 for diamond. Elemental boron is harder than almost anything except diamond.

© Theodore Gray/RGB Research 2006

© Theodore Gray/RGB Research 2006

Elemental boron has several forms. Amorphous boron *(left)* is a dark brown powder, while crystalline boron is brittle and has several colors and structures, such as the black form on the right.

Chemical Properties

Although boron is a simple element, with only five protons and five electrons, it can combine with other elements to make extremely complicated structures in ways that are still not fully understood.

Boron is difficult to isolate because it melts at a high temperature, where it is also very reactive. At high temperatures, boron reacts rapidly with metals, hydrogen, oxygen, carbon, and halides (group VIIA, or 17, elements, such as chlorine [Cl] and fluorine [F]). The atoms in these compounds are held tightly in place by sharing boron's three valence electrons. This kind of link, which involves the sharing of valence electron pairs between two atoms that each contribute electrons to the link, or bond, is called a covalent bond.

The other elements in boron's group, IIIA, or 13, are considered metals, and tend to form ionic bonds, which involve the attraction between positive and negative ions. These group members—aluminum, gallium, indium, and thallium—typically give up valence electrons to gain a positive charge and favor links with elements or compounds with the corresponding negative charge.

Boron's covalent bonds can be unusual. In a typical covalent bond, a valence electron from one atom is paired with one from another atom. This pair is then shared between the two atoms. However, in some cases involving boron, the resulting valence pair is spread across three atoms, two of which are boron. This arises because boron's outer electron shell is not full, so it has the capacity for additional electrons. In the special three-atom bond, each of the two boron atoms uses this capacity to share one electron pair among them and another atom such as hydrogen. This leads to boron clusters that can have twelve or more boron atoms combined into very stable, cagelike structures.

The most familiar boron compounds are borates, which are boron-oxygen combinations. Common, useful examples of these are boric acid and borax, which were discussed earlier.

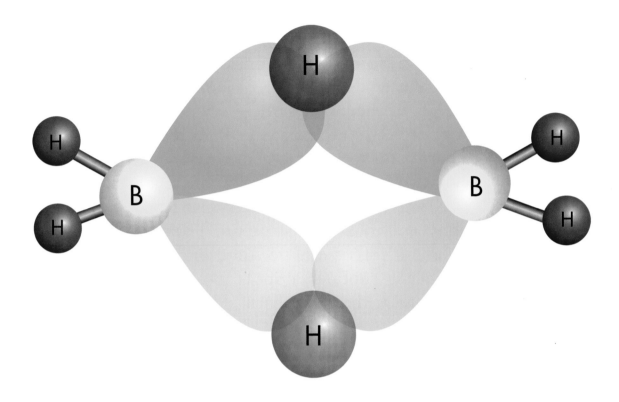

Diborane (B_2H_6) has unusual covalent bonds. Two boron (B) atoms share two electrons (found in the dark green regions) with one hydrogen (H) atom and share another electron pair (light green regions) with another hydrogen atom.

Nuclear Properties

Boron has thirteen known isotopes, each with a unique number of neutrons ranging from two to fourteen. Two of these isotopes—boron-10 with five neutrons and boron-11 with six—occur naturally and are stable, while the rest are radioactive with very short lifetimes.

In radioactive isotopes, the nucleus changes all by itself, with no outside help. This change usually transforms the nucleus into another element, a change called decay because, given enough time, all of the radioactive

Boron's Stable Isotopes

Although B-11 is more plentiful than B-10, the relative amounts of the two isotopes vary considerably from place to place. Our current understanding of boron creation from shattered heavier elements says there should be five B-11 atoms for every two B-10 atoms. Instead, for reasons not fully understood, Earth and the solar system have about eight B-11 atoms for every two B-10 atoms. In addition, small variations from this eight-to-two ratio occur in response to temperature, pressure, acidity, and molecular structure. For example, B-11 in seawater is about forty parts per thousand more plentiful than average, while in continental rocks, B-11 is found at relative levels that are within five parts per thousand of the average.

isotope will be gone. A measure of decay is the half-life, which tells how long it takes for half of the isotope to undergo that process. The radioactive boron isotopes all have half-lifes of less than one second.

Most boron isotopes, including the stable ones, are created when cosmic rays—nuclei and nuclear particles ejected from stars—shatter heavier elements such as carbon, nitrogen (N), and oxygen. Boron is also produced when stars eject carbon, nitrogen, and oxygen nuclei that shatter when they collide with nuclei and nuclear particles. These two processes, called spallation, occur in the depths of interstellar space and closer to home. All beryllium and most lithium are also created this way. The other elements were created when the universe began (hydrogen [H] and most helium [He]), in stars (most of the rest), or in laboratories.

Boron-11 is the more plentiful stable isotope, making up 80.4 percent of the element on Earth, compared to boron-10's 19.6 percent. While

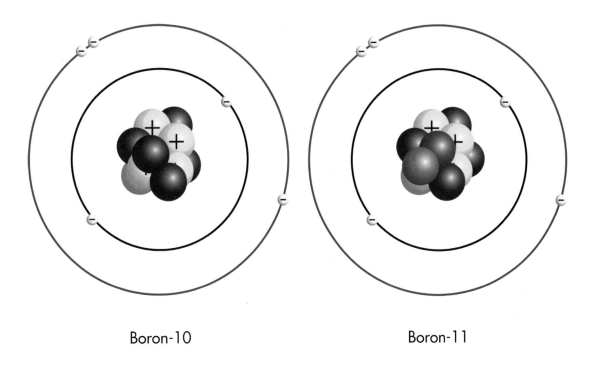

Boron-10   Boron-11

The stable (nonradioactive) boron isotopes have five *(left)* and six *(right)* neutrons (gray and red spheres). About every eight boron atoms out of ten are boron-11, and the other two are boron-10.

most substances containing boron have this isotopic composition, some physical and chemical processes can favor one isotope over the other.

Boron-10, the lighter isotope, is good at capturing neutrons from cosmic radiation or in nuclear reactors. After capturing the neutron, it splits and produces a gamma ray, an alpha particle, and a lithium nucleus.

Chapter Four
Where Can Boron Be Found?

Boron is rare, but its compounds can be found in rocks, soil, and water—usually in small quantities. Large deposits of boron compounds are in Turkey, parts of the western United States, Russia, and in several South American countries.

Commercial deposits of boron minerals are generally found in arid areas with a history of volcanism or hydrothermal activity. Lava, volcanic ash, and hot springs can bring the boron-containing compounds from other rocks to the surface (a process called leaching), where they can accumulate over millions of years, sometimes in the form of borates. The deposits in Southern California's Death Valley took about two million years to form, starting nineteen million years ago. The boron was leached by rain and hot springs from volcanic flows, and accumulated in a lake that eventually dried up to form deposits in this dry region. The deposits were then slowly buried, winding up about half a mile (0.8 km) below the surface. The entire area was uplifted by geological forces about six million years ago and brought near the surface again by erosion.

Smaller amounts of boron compounds may be found in hot springs. Hot springs near Florence, Italy, were a primary source of boric acid and borax for Europe about 200 years ago. In addition to deposits and hot springs, new boron is being created all the time by spallation in the atmosphere, rocks, and water, but in amounts too small to be of use.

Mining and Processing Boron

Today, the mining of borax and related borate minerals is done from open pits, where the deposits are buried a few hundred feet below surface rocks and dirt. Geologists base the pit locations on the mineral type and purity of samples taken from drilled holes. Once a suitable mining location is found, the surface rocks, called overburden, are removed by blasting. In the Mojave Desert mines, the overburden is mostly sandstone.

The Mojave mines are developed with steps, or terraces, in the pit face to keep the walls from collapsing. At the bottom of the pit, giant mechanical shovels about 150 feet (46 meters) high scoop up to 80 tons (73 metric tons; about the weight of 40 cars) of rubble and ore, and dump it into

This giant truck can haul up to about 240 tons of borate minerals, which are dug from huge open pit borax mines and then taken to nearby processing plants. The trucks are usually shipped in pieces and then assembled at the mines.

trucks that can haul 240 tons (218 metric tons). The trucks are 20 feet (6 m) high and 40 feet (12 m) long, and drive on 12-foot-high (4 m) tires.

The truckloads are crushed into one-inch pieces for refining. The crushed ore is mixed in hot water to dissolve the boron minerals, leaving behind rocks and other solids. The borate solution is then pumped to large tanks where smaller solids settle out, leaving the borate-rich fluid floating on top. This fluid is pumped to another tank to cool, causing the borates to crystallize, forming a slurry of crystals and water. The slurry is filtered and washed, and then dried. The resulting borate crystals are stored in silos and domes until shipped elsewhere for further refinement and possible conversion into other compounds and products.

Uses of Boron

Pure elemental boron has few uses, mainly because it is difficult to isolate, except at high temperatures, where it prefers to form compounds. Most of the current applications for elemental boron rely on isotope characteristics.

Borate Mining—Then and Now

In contrast to the highly automated operations of today, borate mining in the late nineteenth century was laborious and tedious. Surface deposits were hand-raked, and underground deposits were shoveled and picked, often in hot desert temperatures that took a toll on the people and animals doing the work. In twenty-day round trips from Death Valley, teams of twenty mules hauled 20 tons (18 metric tons) of refined borate to the nearest train depot. Today, it would take 250 mule teams to move the ore processed in a single day at the borate complex in the Mojave Desert.

A sample of the borate ore borax, also called tincal, is pictured here. It is one of the most abundant borate sources in the world. The largest deposits are found in the United States and Turkey.

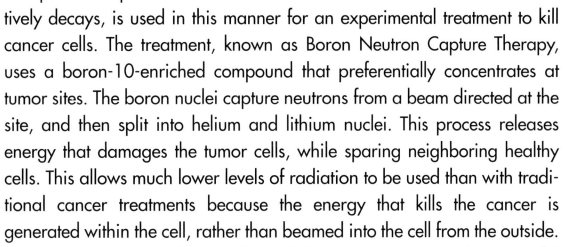

For example, compounds that incorporate clusters of boron atoms have been the subjects of recent intense research because they form three-dimensional structures that may be useful for delivering atoms or molecules to a target such as a cancerous cell. Boron-10, an isotope that captures neutrons and then radioactively decays, is used in this manner for an experimental treatment to kill cancer cells. The treatment, known as Boron Neutron Capture Therapy, uses a boron-10-enriched compound that preferentially concentrates at tumor sites. The boron nuclei capture neutrons from a beam directed at the site, and then split into helium and lithium nuclei. This process releases energy that damages the tumor cells, while sparing neighboring healthy cells. This allows much lower levels of radiation to be used than with traditional cancer treatments because the energy that kills the cancer is generated within the cell, rather than beamed into the cell from the outside.

Boron-11, on the other hand, is indifferent to neutrons, making it useful where the effects of radiation are not desired, like near nuclear reactors. Depleted boron, consisting of boron-11 alone, is used in some glass that protects semiconductor electronics. Boron-10 is excluded from the glass because stray neutrons could shatter the nucleus, releasing particles and energy that could cause data loss and electronics damage.

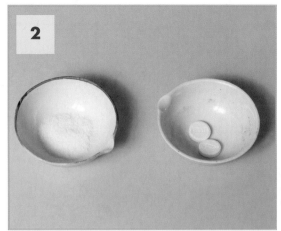

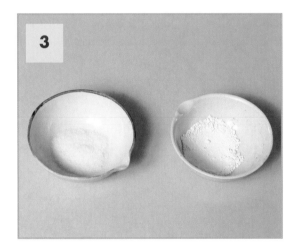

Methyl borate burns with a characteristic color that indicates its electron energy states. Methanol (wood alcohol; photo 1) can be mixed with powdered boric acid (photos 2 and 3) and lit (photo 4) to reveal a distinct green flame.

Boron is one of sixteen essential plant nutrients, vital to a plant's life cycle. Required only in small amounts, boron is necessary in plants to control flowering, pollen production, germination, and seed and fruit development. It also helps to convey sugars from older leaves to new growth areas and root systems.

Important industrial uses of boron in trace amounts include controlling the electronic behavior of some types of semiconductors and increasing the hardness of steel. Amorphous boron, which burns with a brilliant green color, is used in pyrotechnic flares to signal or illuminate and in fireworks.

Chapter Five
Boron Compounds and Alloys

Boron combines with other elements to form compounds and alloys. Compounds always form in fixed proportions, so that boron oxide (B_2O_3) always pairs two boron atoms with three oxygen atoms. Alloys are mixtures of mostly metals that often use non-metals, like boron, to substitute for a small portion of other elements in the alloy. This substitution changes properties of the mixture such as color and strength.

The compounds that boron forms are held together by covalent bonds. In covalent bonding, valence electrons are shared between atoms. The attraction of each atom on the shared electrons is what binds the atoms together. Typically, each valence electron of an atom is paired with one from another atom in the compound. However, in boron compounds made with hydrogen, valence electron pairs are spread across three atoms. The structure of these interesting and unusual compounds—called boron hydrides or boranes—remained unknown until about 1950.

Borates, which include familiar boron compounds such as borax and boric acid, are formed with oxygen. This family of compounds accounts for almost all of the industrial uses of boron. Many boron compounds are also formed with halogens (elements from group VIIA, or 17), metals, and organic (carbon-containing) components.

Borates: Boron-Oxygen Compounds

The most common borate is borax, which is also called sodium tetraborate ($Na_2B_4O_7$). Sodium borate is usually hydrated, or attached to water molecules. Borax that is sold in groceries as a laundry booster is called borax decahydrate ($Na_2[B_4O_5(OH)]_4 \bullet 8H_2O$), formed with the equivalent of ten water molecules. Other useful formulations have the equivalent of five water molecules (pentahydrate) and no water molecules (anhydrate or anhydrous). Boric acid, another common borate, occurs naturally in some hot springs and volcanic areas, but it is usually commercially derived from borax compounds.

Borates are used in laundry and dishwashing detergents, eyewash, and contact lens solution. However, the biggest borate market is fiberglass. Insulation fiberglass provides thermal and acoustic insulation for homes, buildings, and vehicles. Textile fiberglass is used for fabrication of items such as surfboards, circuit boards, and dashboards. Borates are also a key ingredient in heat-resistant glassware familiar under the Pyrex brand name and found in the laboratory and kitchen. These uses, together with enamels and glazes, accounted for 70 percent of the U.S. boron consumption in 2004.

Other borate uses are diverse and can be found in agriculture, wood treatment, metallurgy, automobile manufacturing, and pyrotechnics, to name a few fields. Agricultural uses include fertilizers that satisfy a plant's micronutrient need for boron and pest control that exploits boron's toxicity in high doses to insects and plants. This toxicity is also used as a wood treatment to protect against fungus, bacteria, and insects.

Some borates dissolve and scavenge metal oxides. These properties are used to refine metals by taking away impurities. Borates can also inhibit corrosion and clean metal surfaces to be welded or brazed. Other borates serve as fuels and colorings in pyrotechnics, and as explosives to ignite compounds that fill vehicle airbags when they burn.

Crystallized boric acid has a waxy platelet structure that gives it a slippery feeling, making it a useful component in lubricants, cosmetics, cold cream, and pencil leads.

Borates can tie together long-stranded molecules with repeating units called polymers, an action known as cross-linking. Borate cross-linkers are used to strengthen cement, enhance adhesives, and help recover oil and gas. They are also the basis for such popular toys such as Slime and Silly Putty.

Boranes: Boron-Hydrogen Compounds

Diborane (B_2H_6), a colorless gas at room temperature, has a wide range of applications. It is used in the production of integrated circuits, where small amounts of boron atoms diffused into silicon modify the electrical conductivity. Diborane also speeds up the production rates of some polymers, vulcanizes (cross-links) natural rubber to make it more useful, and is used in the production of hard boron coatings on metals and ceramics. It was once investigated for use as rocket and jet fuels, but boranes never reached the potential thought possible despite intense research throughout the 1950s and early 1960s.

More generally, boranes can convert organic (carbon-based) molecules that are unsaturated (able to react with additional hydrogen) into other

Cross-Linking Use in Oil and Gas Recovery

In oil and gas recovery, the rock reservoir holding the material is fractured by pumping high-pressure fluids down wells. The fractures give the oil or gas a path to the well, where it can be brought to the surface. Cross-linked gels are thick and gluey, and help carry granular material down the well and into the fractures to be propped open.

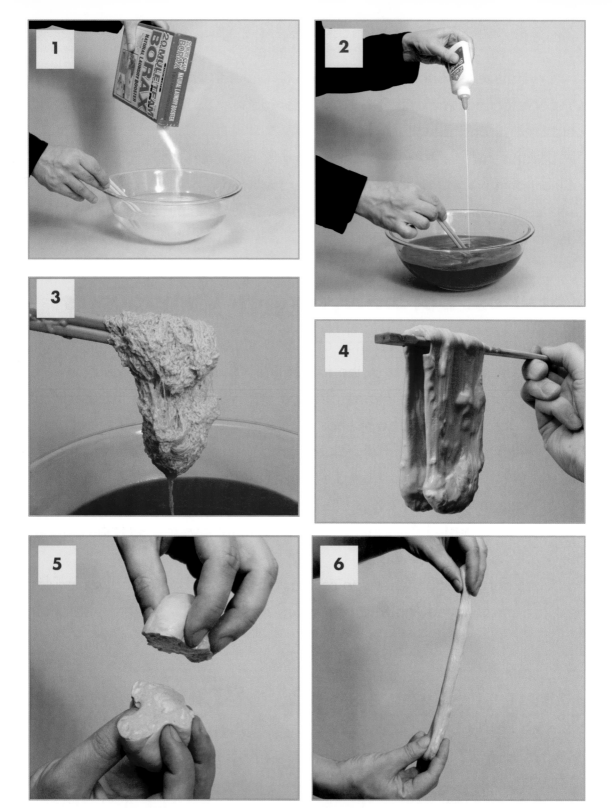

Homemade Silly Putty can be created from borax laundry booster and glue to demonstrate boron's cross-linking properties. (1) Mix the borax in warm water until no more dissolves. (2) Add coloring to the water, then stir while drizzling glue in. (3) Swirl a stick around in the water to collect globs of cross-linked glue strands, and (4) allow the excess water to drain away. The result is a solid that is brittle if pulled suddenly (5) and stretches if pulled slowly or rolled (6).

kinds of organic molecules, a process called hydroboration. This discovery resulted in a 1979 Nobel Prize and has led to inexpensive methods of organic compound production. One of these methods facilitates the formation of an organic compound of a specific shape, while producing none in the form of its mirror-image shape. The two shapes are called optical isomers. This ability to make only one isomer form is important because living things usually produce and use only one shape, and not the other. Before the borane-based method was discovered, the manufacture of medicines with just one desired isomer would usually produce both, which were expensive and difficult to separate.

Other Boron Compounds

Boron combines with nitrogen to form boron nitride (BN), which has three different forms. Cubic BN has the same crystal structure as diamond and is almost as hard. It is used as an industrial abrasive for grinding and cutting metal. Hexagonal BN has a sheet structure, like graphite, and is used for lubricants and cosmetics. Unlike graphite, it is stable at high temperatures. The third form of BN is bound into ball-like molecules. These are being studied for use in delivering medical compounds to cancer cells in the body and for use as a fuel whose bonds store substantial energy.

The ceramic material boron carbide (B_4C) is another extremely hard material, ranking third just below boron nitride and diamond. Boron carbide is used in tank armor, bulletproof vests, and as an abrasive. It is also embedded in aluminum to make a strong, lightweight material used in bicycle frames, for example.

Boron forms other hard ceramic materials with metals in a class of compounds called borides. Borides tend to have high melting temperatures. Metals that form borides include aluminum (Al), calcium (Ca), cerium (Ce), chromium (Cr), hafnium (Hf), iron (Fe), lanthanum (La), magnesium (Mg), molybdenum (Mo), niobium (Nb), tantalum (Ta), titanium

Plates made from boron carbide, a very hard, lightweight ceramic, are used in bulletproof vests and body armor, as well as in tank armor and abrasives.

(Ti), tungsten (W), vanadium (V), and zirconium (Zr). Magnesium boride (MgB_2) displays nearly zero resistance to electrical flow at about 36°F (2.2°C) above absolute zero, or −459.67°F (−273.15°C). Compounds that display this behavior are called superconductors.

Boron compounds with halogens, especially boron fluoride (BF_3), are widely used as catalysts, which accelerate chemical reactions. Halogens are the group VIIA (or 17) elements fluorine, chlorine, bromine (Br), iodine (I), and astatine. Boron bromide (BBr_3) is used in manufacturing fiber-optic cables.

Boron Alloys

Boron hardens some alloys, enhances magnetic properties in others, and is used to protect metal surfaces from corrosion in still others. In small amounts, boron hardens steel, making it more resistant to ductile failure. The boron is usually provided in the form of an iron and boron alloy, which is also used to manufacture the cores of electric-power distribution transformers. In some alloys fused as protective coatings to metal surfaces, boron is included as an alloy component to clean these surfaces.

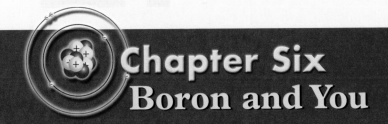

Chapter Six
Boron and You

Boron compounds have been known for at least 1,000 years as ores and from hot-spring waters. Although traditionally used in laundry-boosting compounds, boron shows up in some surprising places, like pie pans, MP3 players, and futuristic electricity sources.

Borosilicate Glass

If you've seen a pie baked in a glass pan, chances are that pan was made from heat-tolerant borosilicate glass. The main ingredients of this glass are boric acid, $B(OH)_3$, silica, SO_2, soda, Na_2CO_3, and lime, CaO. The glass has come to be known as Pyrex, after a brand of borosilicate cookware that was introduced in 1915 by the Corning Glass Works Company. Typical soda-lime glass, which lacks boron, breaks more easily from the thermal stresses that are created when going between room temperatures and cooking or baking temperatures. However, the addition of boron reduces thermal stresses by reducing the thermal expansion of the glass. It also raises the temperature where the glass softens from 1,350°F (730°C) to about 1,500°F (820°C), and reduces its electrical conductivity. Besides bakeware, other early uses of borosilicate glass included laboratory glassware, railroad lantern lenses, and insulators used to suspend high-power electrical lines from poles.

Glass that contains boron expands less when heated, which reduces thermal stresses, and softens at higher temperatures, making it good for baking dishes and laboratory glassware.

Super-Strong Magnet

Many portable devices owe their small size and big performance to strong permanent magnets made from an alloy of boron, iron, and the actinide element neodymium (Nd). The magnets can be found in head-phones, cordless drills, and digital music players. In all of these devices, magnetic force exerted on electricity flowing through wires (which creates a magnet of the wire) causes mechanical motion. This motion can be used to move a diaphragm to make sound in headphones or to spin the shaft in a cordless drill. In music players with tiny, high-capacity hard drives, the motion moves an arm that reads digital music from the disk drive. The greater magnetic force of the boron-containing magnets compared to older types means less electricity is needed. This permits smaller portable devices and extends the time between battery recharges.

Hydrogen Fuel Cell

Boron compounds may help reduce our use of fossil fuels such as oil, natural gas, and coal. Around the world, there is concern about our dependency on these nonrenewable fuels and the climate effects from using them. High-energy boron compounds could help ease these concerns by providing a clean, alternative energy source for electricity and vehicles. One candidate compound is sodium borohydride ($NaBH_4$), which releases its hydrogen when combined with water and run over a catalyst made of the elements ruthenium (Ru) and nickel (Ni). The hydrogen is then converted to electricity in a fuel cell. The by-products are water and the harmless sodium borate ($NaBO_2$), rather than pollutants thought to contribute to global warming. Test models of this borane-based fuel cell have run cars and are being adapted to smaller sizes to power laptop computers and portable electronics for extended durations. This approach has the benefit of being much lighter and longer lasting than metal-based batteries.

Boron is a special element, both in its origins and its amazing range of uses. It is created when cosmic rays shatter heavier elements. On Earth, it concentrates as compounds found in deserts, where volcanoes and hot springs dissolved them from other rocks. These compounds help warm our homes, house electronic components, cook our food, and clean our laundry, to name just a few uses. Chemists have recently been working on boron forms not found in nature. These new forms hold great promise for an even richer array of uses.

The Periodic Table of Elements

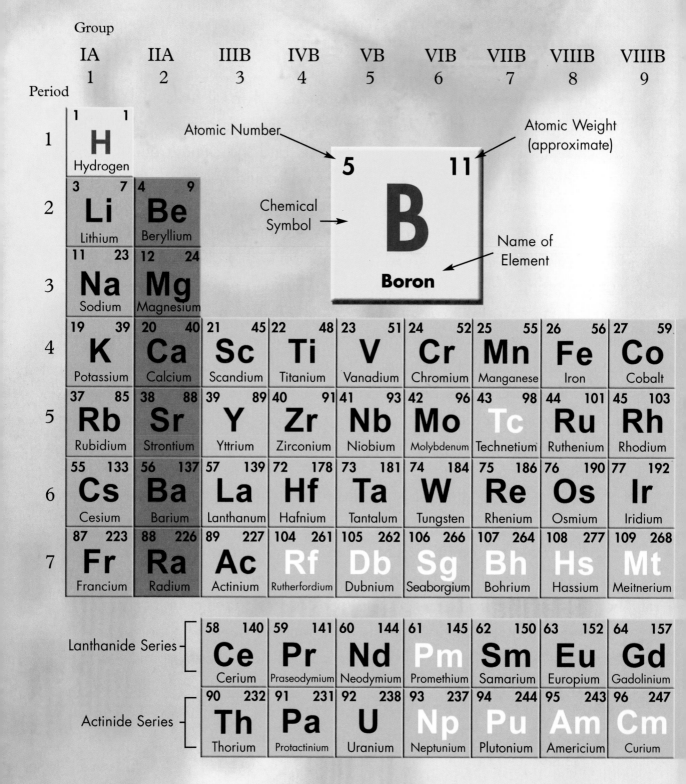

Group

Period	IA 1	IIA 2	IIIB 3	IVB 4	VB 5	VIB 6	VIIB 7	VIIIB 8	VIIIB 9
1	**1 1** **H** Hydrogen								
2	**3 7** **Li** Lithium	**4 9** **Be** Beryllium							
3	**11 23** **Na** Sodium	**12 24** **Mg** Magnesium							
4	**19 39** **K** Potassium	**20 40** **Ca** Calcium	**21 45** **Sc** Scandium	**22 48** **Ti** Titanium	**23 51** **V** Vanadium	**24 52** **Cr** Chromium	**25 55** **Mn** Manganese	**26 56** **Fe** Iron	**27 59.** **Co** Cobalt
5	**37 85** **Rb** Rubidium	**38 88** **Sr** Strontium	**39 89** **Y** Yttrium	**40 91** **Zr** Zirconium	**41 93** **Nb** Niobium	**42 96** **Mo** Molybdenum	**43 98** **Tc** Technetium	**44 101** **Ru** Ruthenium	**45 103** **Rh** Rhodium
6	**55 133** **Cs** Cesium	**56 137** **Ba** Barium	**57 139** **La** Lanthanum	**72 178** **Hf** Hafnium	**73 181** **Ta** Tantalum	**74 184** **W** Tungsten	**75 186** **Re** Rhenium	**76 190** **Os** Osmium	**77 192** **Ir** Iridium
7	**87 223** **Fr** Francium	**88 226** **Ra** Radium	**89 227** **Ac** Actinium	**104 261** **Rf** Rutherfordium	**105 262** **Db** Dubnium	**106 266** **Sg** Seaborgium	**107 264** **Bh** Bohrium	**108 277** **Hs** Hassium	**109 268** **Mt** Meitnerium

Atomic Number

Atomic Weight (approximate)

Chemical Symbol

5 11
B
Boron

Name of Element

Lanthanide Series

58 140 **Ce** Cerium	59 141 **Pr** Praseodymium	60 144 **Nd** Neodymium	61 145 **Pm** Promethium	62 150 **Sm** Samarium	63 152 **Eu** Europium	64 157 **Gd** Gadolinium

Actinide Series

90 232 **Th** Thorium	91 231 **Pa** Protactinium	92 238 **U** Uranium	93 237 **Np** Neptunium	94 244 **Pu** Plutonium	95 243 **Am** Americium	96 247 **Cm** Curium

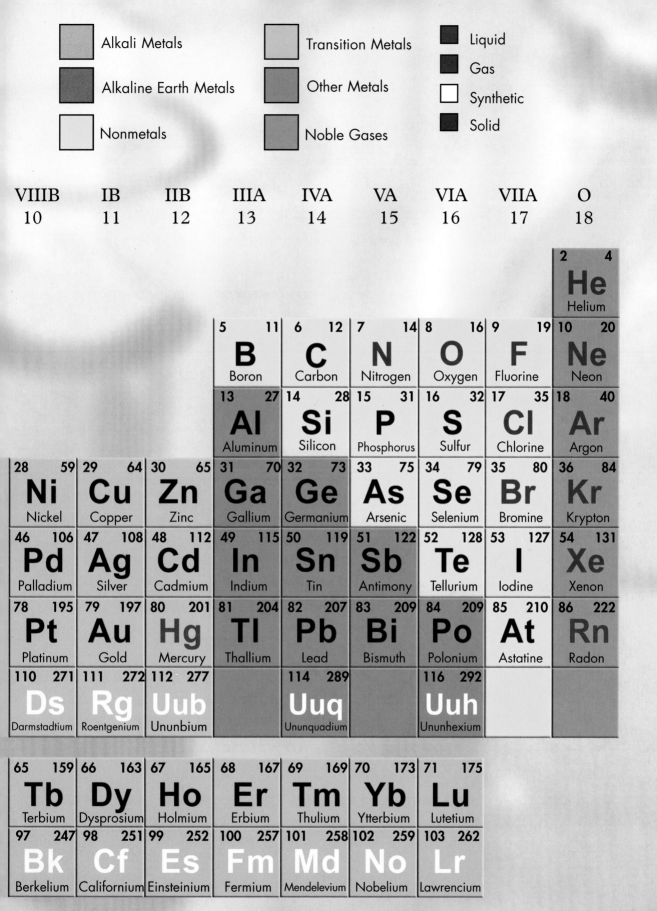

Alkali Metals

Alkaline Earth Metals

Nonmetals

Transition Metals

Other Metals

Noble Gases

Liquid

Gas

Synthetic

Solid

VIIIB 10	IB 11	IIB 12	IIIA 13	IVA 14	VA 15	VIA 16	VIIA 17	O 18
								2 4 **He** Helium
			5 11 **B** Boron	6 12 **C** Carbon	7 14 **N** Nitrogen	8 16 **O** Oxygen	9 19 **F** Fluorine	10 20 **Ne** Neon
			13 27 **Al** Aluminum	14 28 **Si** Silicon	15 31 **P** Phosphorus	16 32 **S** Sulfur	17 35 **Cl** Chlorine	18 40 **Ar** Argon
28 59 **Ni** Nickel	29 64 **Cu** Copper	30 65 **Zn** Zinc	31 70 **Ga** Gallium	32 73 **Ge** Germanium	33 75 **As** Arsenic	34 79 **Se** Selenium	35 80 **Br** Bromine	36 84 **Kr** Krypton
46 106 **Pd** Palladium	47 108 **Ag** Silver	48 112 **Cd** Cadmium	49 115 **In** Indium	50 119 **Sn** Tin	51 122 **Sb** Antimony	52 128 **Te** Tellurium	53 127 **I** Iodine	54 131 **Xe** Xenon
78 195 **Pt** Platinum	79 197 **Au** Gold	80 201 **Hg** Mercury	81 204 **Tl** Thallium	82 207 **Pb** Lead	83 209 **Bi** Bismuth	84 209 **Po** Polonium	85 210 **At** Astatine	86 222 **Rn** Radon
110 271 **Ds** Darmstadtium	111 272 **Rg** Roentgenium	112 277 **Uub** Ununbium		114 289 **Uuq** Ununquadium		116 292 **Uuh** Ununhexium		

65 159 **Tb** Terbium	66 163 **Dy** Dysprosium	67 165 **Ho** Holmium	68 167 **Er** Erbium	69 169 **Tm** Thulium	70 173 **Yb** Ytterbium	71 175 **Lu** Lutetium
97 247 **Bk** Berkelium	98 251 **Cf** Californium	99 252 **Es** Einsteinium	100 257 **Fm** Fermium	101 258 **Md** Mendelevium	102 259 **No** Nobelium	103 262 **Lr** Lawrencium

 # Glossary

alpha particle The nucleus of a helium atom.

borates The name of boron compounds that contain oxygen.

catalyst A substance that speeds a chemical reaction or alters its usual conditions.

electron An elementary particle that has a negative electrical charge as large as the proton's positive charge but that is only about 1/1,836 as heavy.

gamma rays Electromagnetic energy of higher energy and frequency than X-rays.

half-life The amount of time it takes for half of a radioactive substance to disintegrate in a particular nuclear reaction.

neutron An uncharged elementary particle slightly heavier than a proton that exists primarily in atomic nuclei and is present in all known atomic nuclei, except the hydrogen-1 nucleus.

nucleus (plural: nuclei) The positively charged central portion of an atom containing nearly all of the atomic mass, consisting of protons and, usually, neutrons.

polymer A molecule made up of repeating units connected by covalent chemical bonds.

proton A particle that carries a positive electrical charge as strong as the electron's negative charge and is found in atomic nuclei.

radioactivity The spontaneous emission of particles and gamma rays by the disintegration of a nucleus. The term also refers to the emissions.

spallation A nuclear reaction that ejects lighter particles as the result of the bombardment of a nucleus (for instance, as by high-energy protons).

For More Information

Borax Visitor Center
14485 Borax Road
Boron, CA 93516-2017
(760) 762-7588
Web site: http://www.borax.com/borax6.html

Los Alamos National Laboratory
P.O. Box 1663
Los Alamos, NM 87545
(888) 841-8256
Web site: http://periodic.lanl.gov/default.htm

The Nobel Foundation
P.O. Box 5232
SE-102 45 Stockholm, Sweden
Web site: http://nobelprize.org

Web Sites

Due to the changing nature of Internet links, Rosen Publishing has developed an online list of Web sites related to the subject of this book. This site is updated regularly. Please use this link to access the list:

http://www.rosenlinks.com/uept/boro

For Further Reading

Oxlade, Chris. *Elements and Compounds.* Chicago, IL: Heinemann, 2002.

Sacks, Oliver. *Uncle Tungsten: Memories of a Chemical Boyhood.* New York, NY: Vintage Books, 2002.

Stwertka, Albert. *A Guide to Elements.* New York, NY: Oxford University Press, 2002.

VanCleave, Janice. *Chemistry for Every Kid: 101 Easy Experiments That Really Work.* New York, NY: John Wiley and Sons, 1989.

Bibliography

Cavette, Chris. "Magnet." How Products Are Made: Volume 2. Retrieved April 15, 2006 (http://www.madehow.com/Volume-2/Magnet.html).

Columbia Encyclopedia. "Periodic law." 6th ed. New York, NY: Columbia University Press, 2001.

Corey, E. J. "Boron." *Chemical and Engineering News,* September 8, 2003. Retrieved April 3, 2006 (http://pubs.acs.org/cen/80th/boron.html).

Encyclopædia Britannica. "Boron." 2006. Retrieved April 23, 2006 (http://search.eb.com/eb/article-8339).

Freemantle, Michael. "Boron Neutron Capture Therapy." *Chemical and Engineering News,* Vol. 80, No. 34, August 26, 2002, p. 13.

Lyday, Phyllis A. "Boron." Mineral Commodity Summaries 2006. United States Geological Society. Retrieved April 8, 2006

(http://minerals.usgs.gov/minerals/pubs/commodity/boron/
boronmcs06.pdf).

The Rare-Earth Magnetics Association. "Rare-Earth Magnets—Patents
and History." 2002. Retrieved April 10, 2006 (http://www.
rareearth.org/magnets_patents_history.htm).

Romanowski, Perry. "Pyrex." How Products Are Made: Volume 7. Retrieved
March 20, 2006 (http://www.madehow.com/Volume-7/Pyrex.html).

Woo, Cynthia. "Teel's Marsh: Birthplace of a Legend." July 30, 2003.
Retrieved April 30, 2006 (http://www.death-valley.us/article689.html).

Index

About the Author

Rick Adair is an energy policy reporter based in Seattle, Washington. After receiving his Ph.D. in earth sciences from the University of California at San Diego, he worked as a seismologist on a nuclear waste repository project and as a geophysicist on energy and ocean acoustics projects. He then provided programming and analysis for a private planetary geology firm whose cameras have orbited Mars. Adair has been a reporter since 1998, working science and environmental beats for papers in California and Nevada, and is now a writer and news editor for an energy policy publication.

Photo Credits

Cover, pp. 1, 12, 15, 21, 25, 27, 42–43 by Tahara Anderson; pp. 5, 31 © Lester V. Bergman/Corbis; p. 6 © John Bartholomew/Corbis; p. 8 (left) © Hulton Archive/Getty Images; p. 8 (right) © Library of Congress, Prints and Photographs Division; p. 9 © Mark Gibson/Index Stock Imagery; p. 17 © Bettmann/Corbis; p. 23 (left and right) Element photography provided by Theodore Gray & RGB Research Ltd. © 2006 RGB Research Ltd. all rights reserved: see http://www.element-collection.com; p. 29 courtesy of Edwards Air Force Base, by Lt. Col. Sandy Burr; pp. 32, 36 by Mark Golebiowski; p. 38 © Mario Tama/Getty Images; p. 40 © James L. Amos/Corbis.

Special thanks to Jenny Ingber, high school chemistry teacher, Region 9 Schools, New York City, for her assistance in executing the science experiments in this book.

Designer: Tahara Anderson; Editor: Kathy Kuhtz Campbell